Leabharlann Chontae na Mí

3 0011 00003 1386

THREE
ONE-ACT
PLAYS

WITHDRAWN
FROM
STOCK

by

Patrick Fagan

Branar
Dublin

KU-050-016

822FAG/270288

© Patrick Fagan 1983
ISBN 0 9508185 1 8

The plays in this book are copyright. Requests for permission to perform them should be made to the author, c/o Society of Irish Playwrights, Liberty Hall, Dublin 1. The fee for each performance is £4 in the case of amateur groups. Professional terms by arrangement.

Printed by Leinster Leader Ltd., Naas, Co. Kildare.

Copies of this book can be had from the author at 77 Ballytore Road, Dublin 14, or from booksellers.

By the same author:
View from Mount Pelier
(a collection of poetry)

Bíonn an fhírinne searbh
(a collection of short stories in Irish)

CONTENTS

SOW THE
WIND

A Play in One Act

CHARACTERS

MARTIN DOYLE

BRIDIE, his wife

KATE, their daughter

FATHER WILLIE

TOM WALSH (pronounced "Welsh")

TIME: The present.

The action of the play takes place in the kitchen of a fairly well-to-do farmer's house. The time is the present. There is a door at back Right leading to the hall, hall-door and the upstairs. There is a window Right centre looking out on the front lawn and a further window Left centre looking on the farmyard at back. A further door beyond the window Left leads outside to farmyard. This door is open. The table is set for tea.

When the curtain rises, Martin Doyle is to be seen in front of a mirror combing his hair and titivating himself generally. He is in his late fifties but he is still a fine figure of a man. He glances out through window Right when a car is heard coming to a halt outside. Presently Bridie, Martin's wife, enters by door at back Right. She is also in her late fifities and carries a bag containing groceries.

It should be made clear right from the start that there is no love lost between Martin and Bridie. Martin invariably speaks roughly, almost begrudgingly, to her. Her tone towards him is more conciliatory but should give the impression of long-suffering. The impression should be given from the start that there is long-standing friction between the two.

BRIDIE: *[entering by door at back]* **Bad cess to her anyway!**
MARTIN: **And who might that be?**
BRIDIE: **That Mrs. O'Connell. As luck would have it, I ran into her in the Post Office and didn't she insist on me going in to see the baby.**
MARTIN: **I thought you'd be in a hurry home, considering the day that's in it.**
BRIDIE: **Sure I couldn't refuse the woman and it the second or third time she asked me in.**
MARTIN: **Do you realise it's nearly eight o'clock?**
BRIDIE: **Eight o'clock! Isn't it a fret now how time flies.**
MARTIN: **And didn't Kate say they'd be here around eight?**
BRIDIE: **But sure haven't I got everything ready? The salad. The Madiera cake. The table fully laid. And sure you didn't forget yourself to put the kettle on. And I'm glad to see you've washed and shaved yourself in honour of the occasion.**

6

MARTIN: It's a wonder you wouldn't hurry on home in honour of the occasion. Gossiping as usual down the road, I suppose.

BRIDIE: The only one I was gossiping with was Mrs. O'Connell. It's a fine baby, God bless him. And she is as proud of him as if it was one of her own.

MARTIN: Well, Richard O'Connell has a son and heir at last — of sorts.

BRIDIE: It's Paddy-the-next-best-thing, I suppose. They can't have one of their own — so the doctor said. And if it brings them a little bit of happiness, sure that's the main thing . . . Martin, I was often thinking . . .

MARTIN: What were you thinking?

BRIDIE: Ah, it's too late now at any rate.

MARTIN: What were you thinking?

BRIDIE: As I say, it's too late now, but I often thought the solution to our difficulties might have been to adopt . . .

MARTIN: I wouldn't think of such a thing for one minute. It's not the same thing as having a son of your own — your own flesh and blood. And why would we put ourselves out for someone else's mistake? Besides, you wouldn't know what kind of a pedigree a bucko like that might have. No, thank you very much, I'd rather stay the lousy way I am.

BRIDIE: You always had the hard word, Martin Doyle. It's too late now anyway . . . [as she closes the door at Left and glances out to yard] I see you've taken the cover off that ould well again.

MARTIN: I was trying to find out was there much water left in it. We may have to fall back on it to provide water for the cattle if the drought continues.

BRIDIE: It's very dangerous the way it is.

MARTIN: Yerra, there's no danger. Don't we all know it's there?

BRIDIE: But supposing a child was to come in. You mind the fright I got with that same well when Kate was small.

MARTIN: But Kate is big now. Take my word for it, there's no danger.

BRIDIE: Anyway it's a simple thing to put the cover back on it. I don't know what it is but even to think of that well gives me the willies.

7

MARTIN: *[resignedly]* **All right. I'll cover it tomorrow.**

BRIDIE: **Tomorrow! Why can't you do it today?**

MARTIN: **Because I have to make a new cover for it. That's the why. The old one was half rotten.**

BRIDIE: **All right, tomorrow it is. But don't leave it a day longer . . .** *[changing the subject]* **I don't suppose Father Willie will be staying. He'll be hurrying home. His mother isn't so well. So Kate said in her letter.**

MARTIN: **That reminds me. I saw Tom Walsh at Mass on Sunday. I hear he's not going back to England any more.**

BRIDIE: **It's a wonder you wouldn't mention that to a body before now. And he and Kate . . .**

MARTIN: *[interrupting her]* **There's no hurry with the bad news.**

BRIDIE: **God forgive me, but I hoped and prayed that he'd never turn up again.**

MARTIN: **Well, he has turned up again — like the bad penny.**

BRIDIE: **I hope and trust that Kate has put him out of her head by now. Nice state of affairs after what we spent on her education, if Tom Walsh is the height of her matrimonial ambitions.**

MARTIN: **If that's how it is, it's something we'll have to put a stop to.**

BRIDIE: **Easier said than done. You know the youth of today.**

MARTIN: **We'll have to stop it by hook or by crook — by fair means or by foul — do you hear?**

BRIDIE: **I hear you, Martin. But it's easier said than done.** *[A car is heard coming to a stop outside. Opening and closing of car doors etc.]*

MARTIN: **That will be them now.**

(Bridie, followed by Martin, goes out through door at back into hall where they can be seen greeting Kate and Father Willie. Kate is a good-looking girl in her late twenties. Father Willie is aged about forty.]

BRIDIE: *(with some emotion)* **Welcome home, Kate, my child! And you too, of course, Father Willie.**

MARTIN: **A grand céad míle fáilte to you both.**

KATE: *[in kitchen now]* **Dad! Mom! It's great to be home.**

FATHER WILLIE: **Ah, Martin and Bridie, it's fresh and well you're looking. I've brought your daughter back to you safe and sound. But I'm afraid I can't persuade her to do another** stint in Brazil. A pity because she's a first-class doctor and she picked up the Portuguese lingo like nobody's business.

KATE: Oh, it's great to be home again. Brazil was o.k. but after all there's no place like home. And you, Dad, you're keeping well?

MARTIN: I can't complain.

BRIDIE: Won't you take off your coat, Father Willie? And take your ease.

FATHER WILLIE: I have to be off, Bridie. The mother isn't too well at all.

BRIDIE: Ah, the poor woman. I hope it's nothing too serious.

FATHER WILLIE: She hasn't been that good for some time now. Sure, she's getting on in years.

BRIDIE: Aren't we all?

MARTIN: I have a couple of bags of spuds for your brother, Father Willie. They're out in the barn. He tells me there's a fierce scarcity of spuds the year on that side of the country.

FATHER WILLIE: I hope you can spare them, Martin.

MARTIN: Sure, we have plenty.

BRIDIE: Kate, let me help you with your baggage to your room.

KATE: Won't it be great to be back in my own little room again?

BRIDIE: And didn't you have a nice little room to yourself in Brazil?

KATE: Oh, sure! But I missed the birds singing in the mornings like they do here.

BRIDIE: Oh, then you can have my share of the birds in the morning. They have me moidered. I can't get a wink of sleep after five o'clock at this time of year, they kick up such an unholy racket.

KATE: It's the old story. You don't miss something until it is taken away from you.

BRIDIE: [as she and Kate exit] Well, you can have my share of the birds. [to Martin] Martin, will you give Father Willie something to drink?

MARTIN: I suppose you'll have a drop of the hard tack, Father.

FATHER WILLIE: Just a little, mind, I'm driving.

[Martin fetches a bottle of whiskey from a cupboard and pours out drinks for himself and Father Willie.]

FATHER WILLIE: [drinking] Sláinte!

9

MARTIN: Sláinte! . . . Isn't it great weather. Look at that for a sunset. I never saw the country looking so well.

FATHER WILLIE: *(looking out window Left)* Doesn't the country look great in the early Summer. It's you that has the fine place here, Martin. I was looking at it as we were coming along the road.

MARTIN: Aye, there's up to eighty Irish acres in it. Good land, most of it.

FATHER WILLIE: You're a snug man, Martin.

MARTIN: Appearances can be deceptive.

FATHER WILLIE: Fine two-storey house with all conveniences. The best of farm buildings. The most up-to-date machinery, I suppose. Everything Hunkey-dorey, as the man said.

MARTIN: Hunkey-dorey, how are you!

FATHER WILLIE: Haven't you everything a man could want for now?

MARTIN: My one great regret is that I've no son to leave it to — to carry on the name, that is. And I wouldn't mind only the Doyles have been working this farm for generations, for well over two hundred years, in fact.

FATHER WILLIE: And can't Kate settle down here and carry on a practice? One of these days she'll be bringing you in some fine strapping fellow.

MARTIN: That's not the same as a son of your own. You don't know how much I've always wanted a son. But when Kate was born, the doctor told us, if herself had another child, it would put her life in danger.

FATHER WILLIE: I didn't know that.

MARTIN: There's a lot you don't know, Father Willie . . . We didn't get on too well after that. It's not everyone I'd mention it to. And I wouldn't mention it to you only you're a priest. Herself had a terrible fear after that of being put in the family way again.

FATHER WILLIE: That was only natural in the circumstances.

MARTIN: That was before all this talk about contraceptives and family planning. It was no bed of roses, I can tell you.

FATHER WILLIE: But you must have all that well behind you by now.

MARTIN: Yes, I suppose so, in a way. But it's difficult not to feel bitter when I think of all those wasted years. Years without — without love, if you know what I mean.

FATHER WILLIE: Man dear, you're exaggerating a bit.

MARTIN: Not a bit of it. There are times when I feel that my whole life has been wasted.

FATHER WILLIE: Haven't you Kate. Isn't that something? And believe you me, she's one fine girl. A credit to you both.

MARTIN: I'm glad you think so.

FATHER WILLIE: She tells me she has this fella and that's why she doesn't fancy going back to Brazil.

MARTIN: And who might he be?

FATHER WILLIE: A pretty long-standing affair, I'm led to believe.

MARTIN: Is that so now? Well, I can tell you, Father Willie, if it's the same bucko as she had before she left two years ago, he'll never darken my door.

FATHER WILLIE: I'm afraid it is the same fellow. Yes, she did mention that you and Bridie didn't take too kindly to him.

MARTIN: That's putting it mildly.

FATHER WILLIE: The understatement of the year, I dare say.

MARTIN: Why in the name of God would we take to him? The likes of Tom Walsh, is it?

FATHER WILLIE: Martin, I'll say this to you and I'll say no more. We happen to be living in the last quarter of the twentieth century. We have to move with the times. I know Tom Walsh's full story from Kate. You're wronging the lad.

MARTIN: I don't want to get into an argument with you, Father Willie. But it's over my dead body that that fellow will come into this house. And I don't care if it is the last quarter of the twentieth century. Now I think we have exhausted that particular subject. I'll go and get the spuds for you. [as he goes out door at Left] You could be opening the boot of your car.

FATHER WILLIE: Will do. Just give me a minute to finish off this. [Bridie and Kate come back through door at back]

BRIDIE: He's getting the spuds for you, Father Willie, I suppose.

FATHER WILLIE: Aye, surely. I'd better go and open the boot for him.

BRIDIE: You're sure you won't have a cup of tea in your hand. It won't take a minute.

FATHER WILLIE: Sorry, Bridie, I have to be haring off home. I'm late as it is.

BRIDIE: Some other time then.

FATHER WILLIE: Sure. I'll call on you again. I'll be on holidays for some months.

BRIDIE: Well, safe home, Father Willie.

FATHER WILLIE: *[to Bridie]* All the best! *[to Kate]* Keep in touch, Kate.

KATE: *[with secret meaning]* Sure. I'll keep you posted.
[Father Willie exits through door at back]

BRIDIE: By the way, if you go out in the yard, Kate, will you be careful of that ould well.

KATE: Why, what's the matter with it?

BRIDIE: Your father is after taking the cover off it. He says he is making a new cover for it.

KATE: You haven't changed, Mom. You always had a thing about that damned well.

BRIDIE: You'd have a thing about it too, if you got the fright that I got when you were small. You were lucky that I noticed you just in the nick of time. Another second and you were a gonner. *[She wets a pot of tea.]*

KATE: But, Mom, I'm grown up now. I may do silly things but I'm not going to walk into a well. *[changing the subject]* Anything strange or startling around?

BRIDIE: Sure, divil a much ever happens around here. Will you pull over to the table now. You must be famished with the hunger. We've had our tea already.

KATE: *[sitting down at table]* I'm as hungry as a hunter.

BRIDIE: *[continuing with the news]* The O'Connell's have a new baby. They adopted, you know. A fine big, healthy child, God bless him. And the neighbours gave him the world of presents. Mrs. O'Connell was showing them to me only this evening . . . Help yourself there now. I think everything is on the table.

KATE: Sure it's grand, Mom.
[Martin returns through door at back]

BRIDIE: Father Willie seems to be in a fierce hurry altogether. Did he have any news?

MARTIN: *[gruffly]* Divil a news. Where would the likes of him get news?

12

BRIDIE: *[to Kate]* You said in your letter that you're not going back, Kate.

KATE: I've had my fill of Brazil, Mom, although I didn't want to be too blunt to Father Willie's face. It's interesting enough for a start but once the novelty wears off it can be pretty dire.

MARTIN: There's no place like Ireland after all.

KATE: You can say that again, Dad. People here don't realise how well off they are. The sheer poverty of Brazil gets you in the end — the poverty and the hopelessness and the misery.

BRIDIE: It's as well for you to stay at home then.

MARTIN: They never filled the vacancy in the Dispensary, or whatever fancy name they have for it nowadays. You can be sure there aren't many doctors that it would suit.

BRIDIE: But it would suit you fine, Kate.

MARTIN: You could live here with us, of course. And maybe later on we could put up an extension so that you'd have a proper surgery to see your private patients in.

KATE: Don't be thinking of any extension just yet, Dad. I don't know would that job suit me. It depends.

MARTIN: Anyway, it's something to be thinking of.

BRIDIE: By the way, aunt Mary is calling later tonight. She's dying to see you.

KATE: Is she now? That doesn't suit me so well.

BRIDIE: And why is that, pray?

KATE: I have a date, Mom.

BRIDIE: A date. So soon.

KATE: Yes, a date with Tom.

BRIDIE: Tom?

KATE: Tom Walsh, who else. He'll be calling to collect me later on.

[There is an awkward silence]

MARTIN: *[breaking the silence]* We both here thought that you'd have that nonsense put out of your head by now.

BRIDIE: Yes, Kate, you know we always objected to that boy.

KATE: I hate to disappoint you. But I'm afraid Tom and I are as thick as ever. You see, when I went to Brazil and Tom, as you know, went to work in England, we continued to correspond regularly. You may as well know too that last

13

March we spent a fortnight together in the Canaries.

MARTIN: A fortnight in the Canaries with that bucko!

BRIDIE: Taking holidays together, that's very serious, Kate.

KATE: Don't be so oldfashioned, Mom. Sure everyone is doing it nowadays.

BRIDIE: And in the Canaries of all places. That's the youth of today for you. Distance no object. Money no object.

MARTIN: And no holds barred, I suppose.

KATE: To make a long story short, we're going to get married.

BRIDIE: Married! You must be plain out of your mind.

KATE: Why?

BRIDIE: Why, is it? That boy simply isn't suited to you. That's the why.

MARTIN: A school bus driver — or that's what he was before he went off to England — he's not suited to a lady doctor.

KATE: Dad, you're a bit Victorian with your lady doctor ideas. And what's wrong with a bus driver anyway? He's a nice boy, with a bit of culture, which is more than can be said for most around here. He has plans to get a job playing in a band. He won't be disgracing you driving a bus any more.

BRIDIE: But when all is said and done, Tom Walsh simply is not suited to you, Kate. Anyway, he's a couple of years younger than you.

KATE: What's a couple of years? We had all this out two years ago. Your real objection to him is, of course, that he's illegitimate.

BRIDIE: It's not so much that he's illegitimate. But that mother of his. Oh, she was a right one! If it was a decent girl itself now that made the one mistake . . .

KATE: Tom can't help who his mother was. No man can pick and choose his mother — or father, for that matter. Anyway, we're not that high up in the world that we can afford to be looking down our noses on other people.

MARTIN: God knows, I'd be the last to pretend to any notions of grandeur. But a girl, the likes of you, to be hanging around with the scum of the parish. A body would expect that you'd have that much gumption in you. And look how your mother and myself worked hard all our lives, made sacrifices, to make a doctor of you. And for what? Is this our thanks?

KATE: Dad, I'm very conscious of all that you have done for me and truly grateful to you both. But I have my own life to live.

BRIDIE: And it's our bounden duty not to let you make a mess of your life. I don't care what claims you make for this boy. He has the bad drop in him. And it will show sooner or later. You mark my words.

KATE: If he has the bad drop, as you say, it's strange that we saw only the good drop up to now. Look at how he looked after his mother when she was ill. And she was laid up for years before she died. Tom is a nice, kind, understanding person. Not that he ever got much encouragement from anyone around here. Precious few presents he ever got from the neighbours such as you say O'Connell's adopted child is getting. It would never strike anyone, of course, that there is really no difference between Tom and this adopted child.

MARTIN: All I can say is that it's your own life you're meddling with. On your own head be it. You were ever headstrong.

KATE: Yes, that's precisely it. It's my own life that's at stake. I'm going to marry Tom and I'd like to have your blessing on it. But we're going ahead with it anyway.

BRIDIE: And Father Willie — what has he to say about this whole business?

KATE: I've discussed it at length with Father Willie. And he says we are doing the right thing. Indeed, he has promised to marry us.

BRIDIE: Did he now? I suppose he's so long out of the country that he has forgotten what is right and proper.

KATE: I refuse to listen to any more of this. I'm going up to my room. It would do the pair of you a world of good if you could get away from this benighted place and then maybe you'd understand what is right and what is proper. [She goes out door at back suddenly, banging door after her.]

BRIDIE: There she's gone off in a huff now and her tea only half finished.

MARTIN: It doesn't matter about the tea.

BRIDIE: It looks as if there's no other way out. She is going to marry this fellow whether we like it or not.

MARTIN: We can't let her do it. We'll have to put a stop to it

15

one way or another.

BRIDIE: You saw how headstrong she is. It may be as well for us to give in to her — gracefully.

MARTIN: And be the laughing stock of the parish. She, married to that tinker.

BRIDIE: I don't see any other way out. Having that Father Willie on her side puts the kibosh on it completely.

MARTIN: It doesn't matter what Father Willie says. *[with finality]* They are not going to get married.

BRIDIE: It mightn't be as bad as we think. The whole thing might blow over quickly, particularly if they'd clear off to Dublin, or to England.

MARTIN: I say to you again. They can't get married. Can't! Can't!

BRIDIE: What do you mean "can't"? I don't understand.

MARTIN: They say that, if you sow the wind, you'll reap the whirlwind. I'm surely reaping a whirlwind now.

BRIDIE: What whirlwind are you talking about?

MARTIN: You know our married life was never satisfactory after you had Kate. You often refused me. *[From this point on Martin and Bridie are speaking very loudly to each other]* You refused me my marital rights.

BRIDIE: If I did, you know why.

MARTIN: Yes, I know why. In the end I got so fed up with your refusals that I gave up asking. It was only a sham marriage from then on.

BRIDIE: And what has that to do with Kate?

MARTIN: I'll tell you what. When a man is refused his rights what do you think he does?

BRIDIE: How would I know?

MARTIN: If he's a strong, healthy, virile man — if he's a man at all — he'll go elsewhere. And that's what I did.

BRIDIE: You didn't!

MARTIN: I did. God forgive me.

BRIDIE: And who was the woman? — not that it matters much at this stage.

MARTIN: Who was the talk of the parish as a bad woman?

BRIDIE: You don't mean to say —

MARTIN: Yes, I do. Kitty Walsh, that woman was.

BRIDIE: *[incredulous]* You mean *this* Tom Walsh's mother.

MARTIN: Aye, indeed. And I can tell you there was a welcome and a half for me there. No beating about the bush there.

BRIDIE: [sarcastically] Tell me more.

MARTIN: I'll tell you more. It wasn't long until she was carrying. She put the blame on me although there were other fellows involved. I paid a hefty sum to keep her trap shut. The child that was born to her was Tom Walsh.

BRIDIE: You're Tom Walsh's father then?

MARTIN: I can't be certain. As I say, there were other blokes carrying on with her ladyship at the same time. But she always maintained that this Tom had a strong likeness to me.

BRIDIE: And has he?

MARTIN: How the hell would I know whether he has or whether he hasn't?

BRIDIE: [looking closely at him] Yes, there is a resemblance. Why is it I never noticed that before? It's a nice how-do-you-do now.

MARTIN: O.K. It's a nice how-do-you-do. But don't put all the blame on me. There's a fair share of the blame going to yourself.

BRIDIE: So that's why Kate can't marry Tom Walsh. There's blood between them. You'll have to tell her the truth.

MARTIN: There must be some other way out.

BRIDIE: You see how headstrong she is. There is no other way to put an end to this business. You must tell her the truth, the whole truth.

[Kate enters suddenly from door at back]

BRIDIE: Your return is timely, Kate. Your father has something to say to you, something very important.

MARTIN: I'll tell her in my own time.

BRIDIE: You'll tell her now. Now, understand! This business can't be allowed to go on a minute longer.

KATE: [quietly] You don't have to explain anything to me. I overheard the whole, awful business upstairs in my room. I couldn't help but hear it, you were shouting that loud.

BRIDIE: You heard everything then.

KATE: Yes, everything.

BRIDIE: You understand now why you can't marry this Tom Walsh.

KATE: It's not as simple as that.

BRIDIE: Don't you understand? You simply can't marry him. There is blood between you.

KATE: O.K., there's blood between us. But I didn't know that until this evening.

BRIDIE: And what may I ask do you mean by that?

KATE: I didn't know there was blood between us three months ago when we holiday'd together and . . .

BRIDIE: And what? Pull yourself together, girl.

KATE: We were very much in love, Mom.

BRIDIE: Are you trying to tell me you had sex — or what?

KATE: It's worse than that, I'm afraid. The fact is, I'm pregnant.

MARTIN: Oh, my God!

BRIDIE: Pregnant with Tom Walsh's child.

KATE: Yes, Tom Walsh's child.

BRIDIE: God of mercy, have pity upon us. What are we going to do? It's a poor and a hard case. What are we going to do?

MARTIN: For God's sake let us all calm down and maybe we could think straight.

BRIDIE: But what are we going to do? — that's the question. *[The hall door bell rings]*

KATE: That will be him now. *[She gets up to go out]*

BRIDIE: You're not going to bring him in here.

KATE: I most certainly am. We have all just to face this problem squarely together. *[She exits by door back and returns with Tom Walsh, a young man in his twenties.]*

TOM: *[entering]* Hello, Martin. Hello, Bridie.

MARTIN: Don't "Martin" me.

TOM: This is a lovely welcome, Kate. Your father and mother are sure the nicest of people.

KATE: I've been telling them about us, Tom.

TOM: About our holidays in the Canaries.

KATE: Yes, Tom. And what's more to the point, they have been telling me about us.

TOM: Me about us? Will you stop talking in riddles, Kate? What did they tell you?

KATE: I asked you once did you know who your father was.

TOM: And I told you I didn't know. Remember? It's something I never could get out of the mother.

KATE: She was paid to keep her trap shut, I suppose.

TOM: I didn't know it was so important for you to know.

KATE: It wasn't important until this evening. Prepare yourself for a shock, Tom.

TOM: *[with affected laugh]* I'm unshockable, Kate. Who was my father? — the Parish Priest or the Boston Strangler. Or maybe I'm the illegitimate son of a duke.

KATE: This is no joking matter, Tom.

TOM: You sure have a point there, Kate. Right, tell me and get it over.

KATE: O.K., Tom. Your father is . . . my father.

TOM: Let me take this slowly. *[the truth dawning on him]* My father is . . . . your father.

KATE: You're sure you understand now, Tom.

TOM: Good God! Are you sure? *[turning to Martin]* Is this the truth, Martin?

[Martin makes no effort to reply]

BRIDIE: Yes, it is the truth — the solemn truth. And the resemblance is there for all to see.

TOM: *[putting his hands on Martin]* So you are my father. The respectable Martin Doyle.

MARTIN: Take your hands off of me, you scum.

TOM: Scum, am I? If I'm scum, then I'm your scum. But did you every pause to think that it's you that's the scum, Martin? You are the scum that put my mother in the family way and she and I had to endure all the taunts, all the contempt, all the sly nudges, while you walked free, a respectable member of the community. But your repectable days are over, Mr Doyle. The world is going to know what manner of man you are. My mother is going to have her revenge, even if she is in her grave.

MARTIN: You talk of your mother as if she was an innocent girl that I wronged. The truth is that Kitty Walsh was the local . . . *[He leaves the sentence unfinished]*

TOM: *[grabbing him]* The local what?

MARTIN: You know what I mean. Take your hands off of me.

TOM: I don't know what you mean. And if you don't withdraw that remark about my mother, by Christ, I'm going to beat the tar out of you.

MARTIN: Take your hands off of me, I said. I've no fear of you

19

in a clean fight, Tom Walsh, even if I'm twice your age.

BRIDIE: For God's sake will the two of you stop it.

KATE: Please, Tom, come with me and we'll talk it over somewhere.

TOM: I'm not going till I teach this get a lesson he'll never forget.

MARTIN: Come outside and we'll see who is going to teach who a lesson. *[He grabs Tom and pushes him before him through door Left]*

BRIDIE: *[to Kate]* Will you go and get Michael Coffey to try and put between them. The keys are on the dresser there. *[Kate takes keys of car and rushes off through door back. A fight is heard off-stage Left.]*

BRIDIE: Holy Mother of God, pray for us! Our Lady of Perpetual Succour, pray for us! Oh Most Sacred heart of the Crucified Jesus — *[A loud penetrating scream from Tom is heard outside. Bridie rushes to door Left and looks on in horror]* My God, the well! the well! *[Martin appears at door Left, panting and looking extremely dishevelled.]* You've thrown him down the well. You've thrown him down the well, do you understand?

MARTIN: *[sitting down at table]* It was self defence. He was coming at me with the bill hook.

BRIDIE: Is there any way of saving him? If we had a long rope now, there might be a chance for him yet. Kate is gone to get Michael Coffey.

MARTIN: I don't want to save him and I don't care if I roast in Hell for it. I sent him flying into it head first. I hope he's finished. *[uncorking bottle of whiskey]* Christ, I could do with a stiff glass of whiskey. I'm not as young as I used to be.

BRIDIE: *[horrified]* You've killed him — your own son! A fine young man with all his life before him.

MARTIN: Listen. It was him or me for it. You should be glad I was able for him.

BRIDIE: He was your son.

MARTIN: He wasn't the kind of son I wanted. You know that.

BRIDIE: What's Kate going to do about the — the baby now?

MARTIN: You never heard of abortions, I suppose.

BRIDIE: Yes, you have all the answers. You have all the answers — except one. The answer to your conscience.

20

Remember you will have to live with this for the rest of your days in this life and to answer for it in the next — even if you get off scot-free in the Court.

MARTIN: There are people walking around with a lot more on their conscience and it doesn't seem to knock a feather out of them. And talking about the Court, remember you didn't see anything. Just stick to that no matter how the police may quiz you. And I'll have my plea of self-defence ready for them pat. Do you hear me?

BRIDIE: Yes, I hear you. *[There is a pause as she walks to door Left. She stands at door.]* I'm going out now to whisper an Act of Contrition over him. It's the least I can do. And I'm going to say a prayer for you too, Martin Doyle, that God may soften your heart.

[She goes out Left. Martin pours another glass of whiskey for himself. Then he suddenly throws his head down on the table overturning the glass of whiskey. He is sobbing loudly to himself as the curtain falls.]

CURTAIN

Red Wine of Love

A Play in One Act

CHARACTERS

FATHER JOHN MURPHY C.C.

STELLA, the priests' housekeeper

FATHER O'SHEA P.P.

KATHLEEN, a young girl

TIME: The present.

NOTE: *Should the producer find the flashback scene technically too difficult to stage, he/she may adopt the alternative course of staging the play in two scenes, the flashback scene being Scene 1, performed against drapes with spotlights, and the remainder of the play Scene 2. In that event the following modifications are necessary in the script. Stella does not leave the room after the words ". . . I'm speaking out of turn if you like" on page 27 and Father Murphy's speech commencing "the bloody ould hairpin" is deleted. On page 31 the stage direction "A car is heard arriving outside" should be inserted before Father Murphy's speech commencing "Suffering duck!" The lines commencing "The flashback scene fades" and ending ". . . Some priest or other" on pages 30/31 should be deleted. deleted.*

Action takes place in the living room of the Parochial House of a country parish. It is around noon in early September.

There is a door at back Centre leading to a hall where a phone can be seen on the hall table. There is a French window (which is open) at Left. There is a further window at Right looking on to the driveway outside. The room is not short of furniture but there should be a general air of neglect.

As the curtain rises Stella, the housekeeper, is busy tidying the room while Father Murphy is seated on a couch reading the morning newspaper. Stella is a matter-of-fact, no-nonsense type of woman in her fifties. Father Murphy is a handsome man in his late thirties. He is dressed informally in white open-neck shirt and black slacks.

STELLA: *[as she takes empty whiskey bottles from sideboard and places them on table]* **I don't know what the world is coming to at all at all.**

FR. MURPHY: *[as he continues to read paper]* **What's got under your skin now, Stella?**

STELLA: **Sure nothing at all, Father John. Who'd pay any attention to the likes of me?**

FR. MURPHY: **I suppose it's that pile of bottles.** *[He leaves aside* *newspaper and walks across room and inspects bottles.]*

STELLA: That and the behaviour of your friends at the party last night.

FR. MURPHY: Sure you shouldn't begrudge us our little bit of divarsion, Stella. Once our new P.P. takes over we can say good-bye to our parties. The bould Father O'Shea, you'll be glad to hear, has about as much time for parties as Paisley has for the Pope. A strict T.T., so I'm told. I can tell you the party last night will be the last around here for some time.

STELLA: It wasn't so much the party as the carry-on. It was nothing short of scandalous. And the songs ye were singing and the jokes ye were telling, sure the likes of them were never heard inside a Parochial House before. I expected something better from the clergy. I can tell you my eyes were opened last night.

FR. MURPHY: Ah, don't be too hard on us, Stella. *[putting his arm around her]* Did anyone ever tell you you're a great ould hoult, Stella?

STELLA: It's the first time a priest told it to me anyway.

FR. MURPHY: *[pulling her leg in a big way]* You must have been the terror of the land in your heyday, Stella.

STELLA: *(giggling)* Will you give over, Father John. If anyone was to see us!

FR. MURPHY: Sure we're only having a bit of gas. A bit of practice, as the man said.

STELLA: *[releasing herself]* Well, you can go and practice on someone else . . . What am I going to do with these bottles?

FR. MURPHY: Leave them and I'll dump them somewhere. But be sure and remind me of them. If the new P.P. ever saw them, he'd have a fit. By the way, there will be a young lassie from Dublin calling this morning. Kathleen is her name. Something to do with the Legion. She's going around the country trying to set up branches.

STELLA: Kathleen, you say. Kathleen what?

FR. MURPHY: Oh damn! I've clean forgotten her surname. Anyway it doesn't matter. Would you show her in here when she arrives.

STELLA: Very good, Father.

FR. MURPHY: And another thing, Stella. In case I happen to be out, I'm expecting a call from McFadden — on the phone.

STELLA: About what?

FR. MURPHY: What do you think? About that bloody wheat out there. It's in a terrible state after all that rain. I doubt if he'll be able to work the combine in it but we'll have to try. It's something else I want to get out of the way before the new P.P. arrives.

STELLA: If you ask me, there's a lot of things you'd need to get out of the way before the new P.P. arrives.

FR. MURPHY: Now, Stella, you look after your business and I'll look after mine. Like a good woman.

STELLA: I'll speak my mind to you, I will, Father John, even if it means speaking out of turn. And the truth is you should have been at home here looking after your business instead of gallivanting around Salthill for three whole weeks.

FR. MURPHY: I was on my annual holiday. Gallivanting around Salthill indeed!

STELLA: Oh, then, Father, you should have gone a bit further than Salthill if you hoped to avoid being seen and noted. Not one but several people I know were in Salthill in the past few weeks and they all brought back stories of the behaviour of our curate.

FR. MURPHY: Would you care to be more precise now, Stella?

STELLA: Very well, then. You were seen drinking in hotels and pubs with young people of both sexes. And minus the Roman collar.

FR. MURPHY: Minus the Roman collar! Maybe you'd like to see me going into these places in chasuble, stole and full canonicals.

STELLA: Make a joke of it now, Father. But I can tell you it's no laughing matter.

FR. MURPHY: I sure agree with you it's no laughing matter. It's a cause for some concern if a man can't throw off the collar and relax without being the subject of criticism and back-biting by a lot of craw-thumping ould hairpins.

STELLA: It's not so much the removal of the collar as the drinking. Do you realise that you were seen by your parishioners much the worse for drink, to put it mildly?

FR. MURPHY: Drink is my problem and my business, Stella.

STELLA: I'm afraid I couldn't agree with that, Father John. If our curate has a drink problem which he is doing nothing about, it behoves us all as friends to rally round to see how we can help. That's what I think at any rate and you can say I'm speaking out of turn if you like. *[She exits closing the door after her.]*

FR. MURPHY: *(looking out French window)* The bloody ould hairpin! She heard stories, she says. I wonder did she hear any stories about me and ... Kathleen.

[A flash-back scene follows between Kathleen and Father Murphy. The scene should be framed in the French window, special lighting effects being used to convey to the audience that what they are witnessing is a flash-back. Kathleen is a good-looking girl in her mid-twenties.]

KATHLEEN: The sea is quiet tonight.

FR. MURPHY: *[sighing]* It's all so romantic. The sea, the cool, still night and — you!

KATHLEEN: It's such a pity you have to go back tomorrow.

FR. MURPHY: All good things come to an end.

KATHLEEN: End? Never say "end". You can come and see me in Dublin, can't you?

FR. MURPHY: Certainly, I'll come and see you.

KATHLEEN: John, allow me to thank you for the lovely time you gave me for the past two weeks. You were so very nice to me.

FR. MURPHY: Sure a darling girl like yourself, Kathleen, how could I be other than nice to you?

KATHLEEN: Now listen to that for palaver. *[with a proprietary air]* I think that white shirt suits you. Much better than that black thing you were wearing the night we met at the sing-song. Wasn't it marvellous how we met at all! I had been up to the mike singing and when I came back, here was this fine, handsome man waiting for me. I'll bet you don't remember the song I was singing.

FR. MURPHY: Of course, I remember. The Percy French one. "Gortnamona". *[He recites the first verse.]*
Long, long ago in the woods of Gortnamona,
I thought the birds were singing in the blackthorn tree;
But oh! it was my heart that was ringing, ringing, ringing,
With the joy that you were bringing, oh my love, to me.

I'm not likely to forget that song for a long time.

KATHLEEN: It's so beautiful and so sad.

FR. MURPHY: [dismissively] That's life, girl. [changing the subject] Kathleen, there's something I'd like to mention to you. When we first met you assumed for some reason or other that I was a farmer — a strong farmer, as they say — and I must admit I did little to correct that idea.

KATHLEEN: And aren't you a farmer?

FR. MURPHY: Well, I am and I amn't. I've got a small farm, yes.

KATHLEEN: Big or small, it will make no difference to me, John. I'm in love with you and you're in love with me, or so you said the other night, remember?

FR. MURPHY: You shouldn't mind everything a fellow says, especially when he has a drop taken.

KATHLEEN: [hurt] Isn't that just lovely now? You lead me up the garden path, you practically propose to me and now it turns out that you just had a drop too much taken.

FR. MURPHY: It doesn't matter whether I love you or not. I wouldn't be able to support a wife — let's face it.

KATHLEEN: Haven't I told you it doesn't make any difference. Anyway, I can always go out and get work. It shouldn't be too difficult for a nurse to get a job.

FR. MURPHY: My dear Kathleen, there are things I could tell you about myself and you'd drop me like a hot potato.

KATHLEEN: What do you mean? You're not married already?

FR. MURPHY: No, I'm not married.

KATHLEEN: What is it then? You'll have to tell me, John. Maybe, it's not as bad as you think.

FR. MURPHY: It's bad enough . . . Do you know, Kathleen, this is the most difficult thing I ever did in my life?

KATHLEEN: You'd better get it over and done with, whatever it is.

FR. MURPHY: Maybe it would be easier for me if I demonstrated it rather than put it into words. [He takes a clerical collar from his pocket which he puts against his neck]

KATHLEEN: [dumbfounded] Why, you can't be serious! You're not a —

FR. MURPHY: Yes, I'm afraid I am. The cat is out of the bag at last. I'm a priest.

KATHLEEN: Well, of all the . . . It was nothing but a pack of lies from beginning to end. Farmer, indeed!

FR. MURPHY: Not completely. You see, there's a little farm attached to the parish. So, I can kind of claim to be both a farmer and a priest.

KATHLEEN: And what, pray, would your Parish Priest have to say if he knew the carry-on of you here on your holidays?

FR. MURPHY: It so happens that I have no P.P. at the present time. My last P.P. died some months ago. The new man is on the mission in Peru and there's been a delay in him taking up duty.

KATHLEEN: And in the meantime you're having the life of Riley. You should be downright ashamed of yourself.

FR. MURPHY: Why so? If it was a married man that led you up the garden path, you wouldn't be half so annoyed with him — now, would you?

KATHLEEN: There's a big difference between a priest and a married man.

FR. MURPHY: Yes, there's this quite important difference. A priest is free according to the law of the land to get married while a married man is not.

KATHLEEN: You're conveniently forgetting your vow of chastity.

FR. MURPHY: Look, Kathleen. Priests are chucking it in regularly now. It's no longer a nine day's wonder. It's only a matter of time until the law of celibacy goes altogether and then every nice girl's dream will be to be hitched up to a priest.

KATHLEEN: I can't see it happening in the foreseeable future. The hierarchy are dead against it going.

FR. MURPHY: I'm not waiting for the Hierarchy to make up their minds then. I'm well able to make up my own mind.

KATHLEEN: I don't believe it.

FR. MURPHY: Yes, I'm getting out. Definitely. I've been thinking about it for a long time now. I was only waiting for the mother to pass on.

KATHLEEN: I'm sorry for you, John, really sorry.

FR. MURPHY: You need not be sorry for me, Kathleen. It would be far worse if I stayed on leading a life of pretence.

KATHLEEN: But it's not right, John. You know it's not.

FR. MURPHY: Not right! Why do you say that? Because it has been dinned into you that a priest is a little god. To tell you the truth, a priest is a man like any other man. Furthermore, sex. It has been drilled into you that sex is a dirty thing, until you're married, that is, and then, of course, there's nothing more healthy, beneficial etc. etc. than sex and the oftener you have it the better. The same goes for the law of celibacy. If it were got rid of in the morning, you'd have every bishop in the country urging his curates — and any of his Parish Priests that were up to it — to take unto themselves a wife, and telling them that marriage was the greatest thing since the sliced pan.

KATHLEEN: But we must look at facts as they are. Celibacy is still there and no sign of it going.

FR. MURPHY: In that case we should have enough backbone to stand on our own two feet and do what we think is right. *[impulsively]* Kathleen, will you marry me?

KATHLEEN: *[with a nervous laugh]* Poor John, you're such a pity.

FR. MURPHY: *[sharply]* It's no laughing matter.

KATHLEEN: I didn't really mean to laugh, John.

FR. MURPHY: You haven't answered my question.

KATHLEEN: *[humouring him]* Will I marry you? It's a good question, John. But you hardly expect me to give you an answer straight away. Let's say I'll think about it. Isn't that the best course?

FR. MURPHY: I suppose I've no right to expect more. *[with feeling]* Let me hold you in my arms. *[They kiss passionately. Fr. Murphy says the following words slowly and deliberately]* How much better is thy love than wine!

KATHLEEN: My love better than wine? What kind of foolishness is that?

FR. MURPHY: It's from the song of Solomon.

KATHLEEN: It's not the wine of the Mass you mean by any chance?

FR. MURPHY: It's certainly not what Solomon had in mind.

KATHLEEN: But it's what you have in mind, John.

FR. MURPHY: Maybe. Maybe. *[triumphantly]* But for me there is henceforth only the wine of love. The red wine of love.

[The flashback scene fades and Father Murphy is left

momentarily transfixed, gazing vacantly out through the French window. The door opens suddenly and Stella rushes in]

STELLA: Would you ever stir yourself, Father John.

FR. MURPHY: Well, what is it now?

STELLA: Didn't you hear the car arriving outside? Some priest or other.

FR. MURPHY: *[looking out window Right]* Suffering Duck! It's the new P.P., Father O'Shea. As large as life.

STELLA: It can't be. He's not supposed to be here for another few days.

FR. MURPHY: It's him all right. Don't I know him to see, for God's sake!

STELLA: And look at the cut of the place. I haven't even got his bed made.

FR. MURPHY: Yourself and your house! What about me? Those damned bottles — can you get some of them out of the way?

STELLA: What can I do with them? I'm not magic. What about your Roman collar?

FR. MURPHY: You've got the Roman collar on the brain, Stella. If the house was on fire, you'd be asking what about my Roman collar.

STELLA: Still and all —

FR. MURPHY: I'm afraid I'll have to go out and face the foe without my Roman collar. *[Fr. Murphy exits. Stella makes frantic efforts to put some of the bottles back in the sideboard. Fr. Murphy presently returns with Father O'Shea, a severe-looking man in his late fifties.]*

FR. O'SHEA: *[as he comes in]* And this, I take it, is the house-keeper. *[to Stella]* I'm Father O'Shea, the new Parish Priest.

STELLA: You're very welcome, Father.

FR. MURPHY: Yes, this is Miss Kelliher.

STELLA: Just call me Stella, Father.

FR. O'SHEA: Stella it shall be. I'm very pleased to make your acquaintance, Stella. As I was saying to Father, I arrived a little sooner than I expected. A friend had to cancel a seat on a plane and I came in his place at the last moment.

FR. MURPHY: I just remembered, Father, that I have an urgent phone call to make. It won't take a minute.

FR. O'SHEA: **That's quite all right.** *[Father Murphy exits to hall, closing door after him.]*

STELLA: **I'm afraid things are a bit topsy-turvy, Father. We weren't expecting you for a few days yet. I haven't got your room ready either but I'll put your bags up in it. What would you like for your lunch? You must be starving. I have some nice cold chicken or, if you prefer, I can fry you a nice pork chop.**

FR. O'SHEA: **The cold chicken will do fine, Stella. Food doesn't interest me a great deal. Who was it said "man wants but little here below, nor wants that little long"? Goldsmith, I believe. Quite perceptive, not to say a bit uncharacteristic, for a Protestant. I suppose you've been here for some time, Stella.**

STELLA: **For longer than I care to remember, Father.**

FR. O'SHEA: *[in reference to bottles]* **I see that someone has been celebrating.**

STELLA: **Ah, just a little party that Father Murphy gave for the curates around these parts. He's very flahool, is Father Murphy.**

FR. O'SHEA: **Flahool. I'd say he's all that.**

STELLA: **You'll have to excuse me now, Father. I've lots of things to be doing in the kitchen.** *[Stella exits to hall leaving door open. Father Murphy can be seen on phone.]*

FR. MURPHY: *[on phone trying to get the attention of the operator]* **Hello! Hello! Operator. Hello operator.** *[sarcastically]* **Is it yourself that's in it at last? I thought you'd gone to Australia. I've been trying to get Dublin 665873 urgently. I've already got two wrong numbers. Very well then.** *[aside impatiently]* **O God, give me patience! . . . Hello! is that 665873? Is Kathleen there, please?** *[in surprised tone]* **She's already on her way? . . . O damn! that's all I need . . . She has an appointment with me this morning but now it turns out that something else has turned up. However, it can't be helped now . . . No, there's no message . . . Bye, Bye! Thank you.** *[He replaces phone and returns to sitting-room, closing door after him.]*

FR. MURPHY: **Sorry for the interruption, Father.**

FR. O'SHEA: **Parochial business, no doubt.**

FR. MURPHY: **You'll have to excuse the state of the place. We** weren't expecting you for a few days yet. I've been here by myself for some time now since the old P.P. died. Indeed, you might say I've been carrying on on my own for some years now. The late P.P. was an invalid for some years before his death. I have a Parish Committee helping me but I'm afraid nevertheless everything is not as it should be.

FR. O'SHEA: Yes, so I notice. In fact I took a look-in at the church on my way here just now. I must say I was rather shocked by its condition. Why, the place is falling to pieces through sheer neglect.

FR. MURPHY: We did start a building fund some years ago and we have collected quite a bit of money. But we were loath to use any of it until the new P.P. arrived. After all, your ideas might be different to ours.

FR. O'SHEA: I can well understand that but that doesn't excuse the present unkempt state of the church. Dirty altar linen, floor unswept, cobwebs hanging from the ceiling. It wouldn't cost much to keep it clean — now would it?

FR. MURPHY: As I said before, we weren't expecting you for a few days. We had planned to have a general clean-up before you came.

FR. O'SHEA: I suppose that also explains the rather informal dress which you appear to favour. Or perhaps you enjoy going through life looking like a pop singer.

FR. MURPHY: You took us by surprise, Father. Caught us with our trousers down.

FR. O'SHEA: Will you kindly refrain from such coarse expressions in my presence. And let me tell you that I believe in taking people by surprise. It's the only way to keep people on their toes. . . . I hear there's a little farm going with the church here.

FR. MURPHY: [indicating fields through French window] Yes, these few fields out here. I planted the whole place with wheat this year on the advice of the Parish Committee. But as you see we were unfortunate with the weather. It's badly lodged after the heavy rain last week.

FR. O'SHEA: Yes, I was taking stock of it down at the church. It is indeed in a bad state. Why didn't you get it cut before now?

FR. MURPHY: The combine man was very busy.

FR. O'SHEA: Did you make any effort to get him in time? One would think that he'd give the priest some preference. Did you make any effort?

FR. MURPHY: I'm only a short time back from my holidays. I didn't have the opportunity.

FR. O'SHEA: The state of that wheat is indicative of the state of the parish as a whole. Anyway, I don't see what business a priest has with a farm or, indeed, with any other kind of enterprise. The priest is a dedicated person and the less worldly goods he has coming between him and his sacred calling the better.

FR. MURPHY: There's many a Parish Priest around here that wouldn't agree with you in that.

FR. O'SHEA: That's what I think in any event. I see you have a fine collection of whiskey bottles here. Indeed, do I notice one or two brandy bottles.

FR. MURPHY: *[offhandedly]* Oh those. Ah, most of them are there since the late P.P.'s time. As I said, he was an invalid during the latter years of his life and he liked the little drop.

FR. O'SHEA: You don't touch it at all yourself, I suppose.

FR. MURPHY: Well, now and again. On special occasions.

FR. O'SHEA: That's not what I heard.

FR. MURPHY: I don't know what you mean.

FR. O'SHEA: Your reputation has preceded you, I'm afraid. In any event, the housekeeper has just informed me that these are the remains of the nocturnal revels of the local curates. You were so good as to invite them to a hooley here, was it last night?

FR. MURPHY: O.K. Father. If you knew that all along, why did you question me?

FR. O'SHEA: Because I have the right to question you. I'm your Parish Priest, understand. And I don't like falsehood on the lips of a priest, Father.

FR. MURPHY: Did you never tell a little fib yourself?

FR. O'SHEA: Are you questioning me? Listen here. I'm afraid you're a little too long on your own here, doing your own thing. From now on I'm the master here and I will not have my curate indulging in drink. I want your solemn word that I've seen the last of such excesses on your part.

FR. MURPHY: Do you mean you want me to take some

kind of pledge?

FR. O'SHEA: Not exactly. But I do want you to cut down on the drink. Furthermore, I want to see you properly dressed on all occasions.

FR. MURPHY: I'm afraid I couldn't accept that at all. You're not dealing with a raw recruit, you know. I'm nearly forty years of age and if I can't have a drink and let my hair down when I feel like it at my age, it's no day.

FR. O'SHEA: Very well, if that's your attitude. You know, of course, that his Lordship is well aware that you are a man with a drink problem.

FR. MURPHY: I only wish it was my only problem. I didn't intend breaking this news to you for some time, Father O'Shea, but maybe it's as well for me to say it now while I have the opportunity. *[in level tones]* I won't be staying with you very long.

FR. O'SHEA: What do you mean? Have you got a transfer?

FR. MURPHY: I mean I'm baling out.

FR. O'SHEA: You can't be serious.

FR. MURPHY: But I am — terribly serious.

FR. O'SHEA: But you can't leave the priesthood just like that. Remember thou art a priest forever.

FR. MURPHY: More old hat!

FR. O'SHEA: *[musingly]* There I was in the wilds of Peru thinking that there was more need for me there than at home in Ireland. And all the time the parish here was in the hands of a priest like you. Island of saints, God help us! *[in a more conciliatory mood]* Well, maybe things are not quite as bad as you think. I have great belief in the efficacy of prayer. Why don't you and I go down to the chapel and say a prayer to God and His Blessed Mother that He'll give you the grace to overcome your ordeal.

FR. MURPHY: I'm afraid the time for prayer is past. My mind is made up. In fact I've already drafted a little message here bidding farewell to my flock. *[takes piece of paper from his pocket and hands it to Father O'Shea]*

FR. O'SHEA: *[reading through quickly with mounting incredulity]* "When this message is being read to you, I will have ceased to be a priest in this parish as I regret to say I'm leaving the priesthood. This, I know, will cause pain to many and perhaps scandal to some. But you must appreciate that the step I have taken was no easy one for me. Believe me, I've taken it only after mature consideration and great anguish of mind. My conscience feels easier now and I honestly believe that I've done the right thing and that it's God's will."

FR. MURPHY: That's it. Perhaps you would do me the favour of reading it from the altar some Sunday.

FR. O'SHEA: You're not serious! You mean me to read this scandalous concoction to the congregation during Holy Mass. I most certainly will not.

FR. MURPHY: Why, what's the matter with it?

FR. O'SHEA: What's the matter with it! You are trying to rationalise this appalling defection of yours and to pretend it is the will of God. If your conscience is easy, then all I can say is that you must have a mighty peculiar conscience.

FR. MURPHY: [sarcastically] Wouldn't life be very simple for me now if I had a conscience like yours. I'd be certain of everything. I'd have no doubts about anything. Everything would be clear as crystal. But that's not how I am. I was ever afflicted with an enquiring mind and the more I questioned the more it was borne in on me that there were certain things that I could not accept.

FR. O'SHEA: You know, you're quite wrong in assuming that I was always certain of everything, that I had no doubts and that I was never tempted. Of course, I had doubts. Of course, I was tempted. But I prayed. I prayed to God and His Holy Mother and they did not fail me. I did not succumb to the temptation and I came out of it stronger in faith than I ever was. Praise be to God.

FR. MURPHY: What you're saying is that you didn't allow yourself to think. When you felt yourself thinking you eliminated the thought root and branch, choked it with prayers, killed it with pious aspirations. As time went on your mind ceased to think and temptation, as you call it, ceased to bother you. Your reason, that great God-given gift, you have set at nought.

FR. O'SHEA: I refuse to continue to listen to this sermon. Conscience — look at where it has got you. You can have your conscience, and the mental torture, the regret and the

36

heart-break as well. A priest without faith, without hope, without Christ. In the name of God, Father, won't you come down to the chapel and we'll both go down on our knees before the Tabernacle. Maybe it's the last chance you'll get to listen to the will of God.

FR. MURPHY: I won't go. I've already told you the time for prayer is past. The die is cast.

FR. O'SHEA: *[trying a differnt line]* Is there a woman?

FR. MURPHY: Yes, there is a woman.

FR. O'SHEA: Well, I'll be — ! I thought the likes of this only happened in South America. Who is she?

FR. MURPHY: She's a girl I met on holidays. You need not question me any further about her because I am not prepared to give you any further information.

FR. O'SHEA: I really don't know what to say. I really don't. I'll have to report all this to his Lordship, of course. I must go down to the chapel. I must do some deep thinking. *[Father O'Shea goes out through hall. After a pause Stella comes in.]*

STELLA: That young girl from Dublin, Father. She arrived about five minutes ago. I showed her into the study.

FR. MURPHY: Father O'Shea didn't see her then as he went out.

STELLA: No. Why?

FR. MURPHY: Never mind, Stella. Show her in.

[Stella exits and returns almost immediately with Kathleen and then withdraws.]

FR. MURPHY: *[shaking hands with Kathleen]* You're very welcome, Kathleen. We're all upside down here. Our new P.P. has descended on us suddenly. I tried to phone you but you were already on the road here.

KATHLEEN: Poor John, you have your troubles, haven't you?

FR. MURPHY: I won't have them much longer. I'm baling out. I've just told his Nibs. He nearly had a fit.

KATHLEEN: You certainly don't believe in wasting any time. I hope you didn't do anything rash, John.

FR. MURPHY: My only regret is that I didn't do it years ago. If I only had the backbone to stand up to my mother. *[with great venom]* The bloody bitch.

KATHLEEN: That's no way to speak of your mother, John. After all anything she did, she did it for your good — or

37

thought she did.

FR. MURPHY: She did it to bolster up her own self-esteem. A priest in the family was what she wanted and I was the sacrificial victim on the altar of family pride. And she was so blinded by her own conceit that she never realised what she did to me. It never once occurred to her that I might be unhappy, that I was driven to drink as a refuge from my loneliness and unhappiness, that I was condemned to a life of celibacy when what I really wanted was a wife and kids and the happiness and security of a home. But she went her unthinking way, blind to everything but the all-consuming fact that she had given a priest to God. And she went to her grave never once suspecting what a hell upon earth she had condemned me to.

KATHLEEN: Why didn't you talk to her, explain to her how you felt?

FR. MURPHY: Easier said than done. It's a problem in communications I suppose. I just could not bring myself to broach the subject to her. I preferred the cowardly way out, if you like, of waiting for her to die. But she lived a lot longer than I had bargained for. She's gone now, thank God, and I'm going to order my life my own way. Do you remember the last night we were together, Kathleen — I asked you to marry me and you said you'd think about it.

KATHLEEN: I have thought about it, John.

FR. MURPHY: Well?

KATHLEEN: I have thought about it a great deal. And I've called on you today for the sole purpose of talking things over with you. You know that I come of what used to called strong farmer stock. I've an uncle a Parish Priest. You can just imagine the opposition there would be to me marrying an ex-priest. They'd think it was the end of the world. It would kill my mother, I'm certain.

FR. MURPHY: I realise that you must take the feelings of your parents and relations into account. But it was never my intention that we should take the plunge straight away. Indeed I well know that in the circumstances it is desirable to wait a decent interval.

KATHLEEN: But there's also the matter of my own conscience.

FR. MURPHY: I don't see that there is any great problem of

conscience for you. The decision to leave the priesthood is mine — O.K.? You've no hand, act or part in it. I had decided on that course long before I met you. When I'm properly laicised and the Church authorities agree to me going, I'll then be in the same position as any other layman and quite free to marry in the eyes of the Church.

KATHLEEN: I know all that, John. But old prejudices die hard. And having it dinned into one for so long about the sacredness of the priestly calling, it's a bit difficult to accept all of a sudden the "about turn" position. Another thing, John, I went to confession recently and told the priest of my connection with you. He asked if you were still in the priesthood and when I said "yes" he asked me to sever all connection with you instantly. [tearfully] He said that marriage to you would not bring me happiness, that the blessing of God could not be upon such a marriage.

FR. MURPHY: Extraordinary theology, I must say. You obviously went to the wrong confessor.

KATHLEEN: That's what he said at all events, John. I've also been thinking of your drinking.

FR. MURPHY: I didn't know you knew I was a heavy drinker.

KATHLEEN: I must confess that I made a few private enquiries and I was told that you have a drink problem.

FR. MURPHY: You mean you went behind my back.

KATHLEEN: It seemed prudent to make a few enquiries.

FR. MURPHY: And you found out that I'm known as a man with a drink problem. Of course, I have a drink problem. I'm bloody nearly an alcoholic. But my drink problem derives simply and solely from the fact that I've been compelled to live an unnatural existence.

KATHLEEN: Maybe so. But how do I know that you'll be able to change your drinking habits if your other problem is solved? Remember I'd be taking you for better or for worse. And there's always the possibility that later on in your life remorse might set in. Marriage might become repugnant to you and I'd be left high and dry. All in all, I think it might be better for us both if we call it a day — don't you think so?

FR. MURPHY: [pleading with her] Kathleen, if you only knew how much I love you. I cannot live without you.

KATHLEEN: You'll get over it, John. They say time is a great healer. There's plenty of other fish in the sea.

FR. MURPHY: Is that all you have to say to me after what we meant to each other. Remember our nights together in Salthill. Remember how we —

KATHLEEN: But that was before you told me you were a priest. Anything I said before that doesn't really count, does it?

FR. MURPHY: But I'm still the same man. I have the same loves, hates, faults, virtues. I look the same. The fact that I'm a priest should not matter.

KATHLEEN: I'm afraid it does to me. Call it prejudice if you like, or superstition. *[moving to go]* I really don't think there's any point in pursuing this conversation any further, John. Let us part as friends. You may think that what I'm doing now is callous and cruel but you may thank me for it in years to come. *[She holds out her hand but he refuses to take it. Instead he turns his back upon her.]* **Well, goodbye, John, and God bless you.** *Exit Kathleen. Presently a car is heard starting up outside.]*

FR. MURPHY: *[going to window Right and looking out after her]* She's gone. That's women for you. They come into your life, you fall in love with them and then quite suddenly they change their minds. They rationalise their actions with a stock-in-trade of well-worn cliches. Time is a great healer. There's plenty of other fish in the sea. You'll thank me for it yet. O Christ, what will I do now? What did Father O'Shea say — a priest without faith, without hope, without Christ ... Yes, I know what I'll do. By God, that would solve everything. As the man said, a consummation devoutly to be wished.

[He sits down on the couch in utter dejection. Presently the telephone in the hallway begins to ring. The ringing continues but Fr. Murphy pays no heed to it. At last Stella appears in the hall and answers it.]

STELLA: **Parochial House ... This is Stella speaking, Mrs. Griffin ... Oh the poor man and he had a stroke before ... I'm very sorry now, Mrs. Griffin ... Yes, Father Murphy is here ... Yes, I'll tell him how bad your husband is ... Yes, I'll tell him it's urgent ... Goodbye now and God bless.** *[She puts down the phone and comes in.]* **That was Mrs. Griffin**

40

from Hilltown. Her husband has had a stroke and he's not expected to last. She asked for you to come as quickly as possible. Father John, do you hear me? The poor man is not expected to last. What on earth is the matter with you. Do you hear me?

FR. MURPHY: Yes, I hear you. I'm not deaf.

STELLA: You've been crying. What happened to you? I never saw you crying before. Was it that argument you had with Father O'Shea? I could hear your voices in the kitchen. *[going to hall and returning quickly]* The little case with everything for a sick call is here, packed and ready as always. All you have to do is get the Host from the chapel. Stir yourself, Father. Didn't I tell you it was urgent. The poor man is at death's door.

FR. MURPHY: Tell that to Father O'Shea. He's in the chapel.

STELLA: And what's the matter with you — are you sick or what?

FR. MURPHY: I've baled out. Chucked it in.

STELLA: Baled out! — what on earth do you mean?

FR. MURPHY: I've left the priesthood. Give your message to O'Shea.

STELLA: Lookit here, Father John, it's well you know the Griffins live in an out of the way place at the other end of the parish. A stranger like Father O'Shea would have difficulty finding his way there.

FR. MURPHY: He has a tongue in his head, hasn't he?

STELLA: Listen here, Father. This man is at death's door. There can't be any delay. Do you hear?

FR. MURPHY: I tell you the poor man would be better off without me.

STELLA: You well know what offerings the Griffins give. Ten pounds, every Christmas and Easter. The least you might do is to attend to him on his death-bed.

FR. MURPHY: Go and tell that to Father O'Shea. He'll be getting the lion's share of the offerings from now on.

STELLA: Listen here, Father. You've reached the pass you're in through your drinking and carousing. *[with emphasis]* If you don't go without further delay, I'll pick up that phone and I'll tell Mrs. Griffin that you're here and that you've refused to go to her husband. Now, for the last time, are you going

41

or not?

FR. MURPHY: *[resignedly]* **O.K. I'll go. Give me the bag.** *[Stella hands him the case. He takes his jacket from back of chair and puts it on.]*

STELLA: **Aren't you forgetting something, Father John?**

FR. MURPHY: *[sarcastically]* **Don't tell me, Stella. It just has to be my Roman collar.**

STELLA: **That's right. Make game of it. You're surely not going out on a sick call without it.**

FR. MURPHY: **You'll be glad to hear I have a spare one out in the car — along with the other gear.**

STELLA: **Well, don't forget to put it on. And by the way, if McFadden calls while you're away, what will I tell him?**

FR. MURPHY: *[absentmindedly]* **McFadden? Oh, McFadden.**

STELLA: **The combine man — about that wheat. What am I going to tell him?**

FR. MURPHY: *[with deliberation]* **Tell him — tell him I'll give him a call tomorrow morning.**

[Fr. Murphy goes out the door with the case in his hand.]

STELLA: *[looking after him through window Right]* **Leaving the priesthood, is it? It's that young strap from Dublin, I'll go bail.**

CURTAIN

THE COUNTRY GIRLS

A Play in One Act

CHARACTERS

KATE

ANN

MICHAEL

MOLLIE

MARGARET

TIME: The present.

SCENE 1

*The action of the play takes place in the living-room of a Dublin
flat which three girls from the country are sharing. The room is
reasonably well furnished with a couch, two easy chairs, a dining
table, a television set and some ordinary chairs. There is a door
Right leading to landing and two bedrooms which are part of the
flat. There is a door Left leading to kitchenette. There is a window
at back with a not very pleasant view of city roof tops.*

*When the curtain rises, there is no one on stage but Ann can be
heard in kitchenette singing a snatch of "I know where I'm going"
to the accompaniment of the rattle of pots and pans and other
kitchen noises. Kate enters presently from door Right. She is a
pleasant, reasonably attractive girl in her late twenties. She wears
jeans.*

KATE: *[excitedly]* **Ann, Ann, where are you?**
ANN: *[off]* **Here in the kitchen.** *[She enters from kitchenette. She
is a pleasant, plain looking, settled girl of about thirty.]* **What's
all the excitement about?**
KATE: **You'd never guess what happened in the office today.**
ANN: **I'm glad to hear something happened. My big problem is
that nothing ever happens.**
KATE: **It's not exactly that anything happened. It's just that
your man, Michael — you know him. —**
ANN: **You mean that budding playwright. I'm all ears, Kate.**
KATE: **It's nothing romantic, Ann. I hate to disappoint you.**
ANN: **And I thinking that the bould Michael had suddenly —**
KATE: **Ah, have a bit of sense, Ann.**
ANN: **O.K. Well then then what happened that has you so
worked up?**
KATE: **Michael came into the typing pool this morning and
started one of high-falutin' conversations on the drama —
you know, that fellow talks about nothing else — and he
was making the point that a play can be written about any
subject, no matter how commonplace. So then, I don't
know what got into me, but I ups and challenges him to
write a play about the three of us here in the flat.**

ANN: And no doubt he accepted the challenge.

KATE: Right first time, Ann. And in order to write this master-piece, he says he'll have to come and see us.

ANN: Well, it's one way of inviting yourself in somewhere. When might he be coming?

KATE: If I know the same Michael, he won't let the grass grow under his feet for long.

ANN: I don't know how Mollie is going to react to him coming.

KATE: Ah, bother Mollie!

ANN: "Bother Mollie" is right. It's a pity you haven't the courage to say that to her face.

KATE: Now, Ann, speak for yourself. You well know that the same Mollie has the two of us rightly tied to her apron strings.

ANN: Personally, I don't think she affects me that much one way or the other.

KATE: Can't you see that we're just going to seed here and Mollie is the prime cause of it.

ANN: Maybe so. But, on the other hand, maybe we'd just go to seed anyway.

KATE: Whatever about you, Ann, I don't think I was cut out by nature to be an old maid. And I really blame Mollie for keeping us the way we are. She just wants us to be in the same boat as herself.

ANN: Are you not exaggerating now, girl? After all if you want to get the odd romance going, Mollie won't get in your way.

KATE: Won't she now? And what about this rule we have about not bringing our men friends into the flat? How am I supposed to do any serious kind of a line with a fellow if I can't take him in here to entertain him? And that rule was Mollie's idea. Old dog-in-the-manger doesn't want a man herself nor does she want anyone else to have one.

ANN: But when all is said and done, Kate, you have the remedy in your own hands. Far be it from me to suggest that you should leave — it's the last thing I'd want — but you must realise that remedy is wide open to you.

KATE: And that's just what Mollie would like to see me doing. It has been quite clear to me for some time now that she has no time at all for me. Rotten snob! Thinks because she's a national teacher that she's a cut above the rest of us. And since she found out that my poor unfortunate father is only a postman, she can just barely tolerate me.

ANN: Now, Kate you're just imagining things. You're far too touchy.

KATE: I'm not imagining things at all. Rotten snob! Always trying to give the impression that her people were really upper crust.

ANN: [dismissively] Upper crust! Sure, her father and mother were only schoolteachers.

KATE: You know as well as I do that that was something out in the heart of the country until very recently. And all that old bull about the servant girls they used to have when she was small. You'd think they were really very exalted people altogether.

ANN: Well, I suppose we all have our own faults and our own virtues. And speaking of virtues, look at how charitable Mollie is. Look at the amount of time she spends in that girls' club, for all the thanks she ever gets for it.

KATE: I suppose it makes her feel important to be able to boss the unfortunate girls around down there. Does wonders for her morale, as she'd say herself.

ANN: Poor old Mollie could do nothing good in your eyes, Kate. [hall door bell is heard ringing] Who can that be now?

KATE: I'll go and see. [Kate exits through door Right. In the meantime Ann busies herself tidying up the room, in expectation of a visitor.]

KATE: [coming back with Michael, a brash, extrovert man in his early thirties] Michael is here, Ann.

ANN: You mean our playwright friend.

KATE: Yes, large as life. Or should I say, larger than life? Michael, this is Ann.

MICHAEL: Hi, Ann.

ANN: You're welcome, Michael. Kate mentioned that you might be coming.

KATE: I was telling her about that famous play I dared you to write. But we weren't expecting you quite so soon.

MICHAEL: Yes, I thought you wouldn't. But the way I look at it, if I am to write that play, I must see you the way you really are, I mean to say without the outward veneer which people assume as a public face. That's why I wanted to take you by surprise more or less, to drop in on you before you had a chance of making any preparations. One other thing, I'll be asking you questions from time to time — questions which perhaps you mighn't like to answer — and I'd like to get true and honest replies. *[Suddenly]* O.K., Ann, what age are you?

ANN: There's no secret about that. I'm thirty-one.

MICHAEL: *[Takes out notebook and writes]* Thirty-one. I like to note down particulars like this or I'd forget them. Occupation?

ANN: Shop assistant.

MICHAEL: Where do you come from?

ANN: Roscommon.

MICHAEL: Father's occupation?

ANN: Farmer.

MICHAEL: And you, Kate. I know you're in your late twenties, that you come from Mayo and that you're a typist in the civil service. But I've never heard you speak of your people. Now, father's occupation, please?

KATE: There's no mystery about it. He's a postman.

MICHAEL: *[writing]* Postman, and no mystery about it. Now, pastimes and hobbies? You, Ann?

ANN: Nothing wildly exciting. Reading, walking, the telly, the theatre now and again.

KATE: Ann is a great reader. A regular bookworm.

ANN: I'm afraid my taste is rather low brow. Mostly thrillers and detective stories.

MICHAEL: And you, Kate? Pastimes and hobbies?

KATE: The same as Ann, more or less — except for the reading.

MICHAEL: *[writing]* The same more or less. Well, what about dances, discos and such like?

KATE: Now and then we go to the disco in the tennis club down the road.

MICHAEL: The two of you go?

ANN: Yes, just the two of us. Mollie, of course, never goes. She wouldn't be found dead in such places.

MICHAEL: I take it that Mollie is the third girl staying here. And why has she such an aversion to dancing, pray?

KATE: She says she has no desire to be mauled and kicked around by a lot of uncivilised drunks.

ANN: There are times when I wonder if she isn't right.

MICHAEL: She sounds like a proper has been, she does.

KATE: You can say that again.

MICHAEL: Well, now, you must meet some eligible men at these dances.

ANN: Eligible, how are you! How naive can you get, Michael? Ninety per cent of the men you meet at dances have no idea in the wide world of getting married — I'm speaking of the ones that aren't married already.

KATE: Gay bachelors, playing the field trying to lure young girls on. You must know the score yourself, Michael.

MICHAEL: You must meet the odd decent fellow now and again, Kate.

KATE: If that miracle ever happened and if we embarked on a serious line, I couldn't take him in here to entertain him.

MICHAEL: And why is that?

ANN: Because we have a rule in the flat against bringing in men — that's to say, a man we might be doing a line with. We can, of course, bring in our brothers and other male relations.

MICHAEL: I realise, of course, that men friends can be the cause of friction between girls in a flat. All the same, isn't this rule going beyond the beyonds?

ANN: It's not all that unreasonable. To tell the truth, if there are three girls sharing and if they are all bringing in their boy friends, it's precious little privacy that any of them has.

MICHAEL: All the same, this Mollie strikes me as a right misogynist. *[The hall-door is heard closing down stairs]* In the name of God, how does she expect you to have any chance of getting a man, if you can't bring him in here.

KATE: Keep it low, Michael. That will be her now.

[Enter Mollie. She is a very well preserved woman in her forties, quite good-looking in a prudish way.]

MOLLIE: Good evening, all.

KATE AND ANN: *[together]* Good evening, Mollie.

MOLLIE: *[referring to Michael]* And with whom have I the honour?

ANN: Mollie, this is Michael. He's a friend of Kate's.

MOLLIE: Friend? How do you mean?

KATE: He's not a friend in that sense. He's only working with me.

MOLLIE: But all the same —

MICHAEL: I can explain everything, Mollie.

MOLLIE: Don't "Mollie" me on such a short acquaintance, please. Miss Dolan to you.

MICHAEL: All right, Miss Dolan — if that's how you want it.

MOLLIE: Believe you me, that's how I want it.

KATE: Listen, Mollie, things are not as you think. Michael is simply working with me. There is no other connection, good, bad or indifferent.

MOLLIE: And pray, why is he here?

MICHAEL: Because I'm a playwright in my spare time and Kate made a bet with me that I couldn't write a play about the three of you here. That's why I came here — to get the lowdown on the three of you.

MOLLIE: You mean to say you're going to write a play about us! Of all the cheek!

MICHAEL: I won't actually use your names.

MOLLIE: Big deal.

MICHAEL: And I'll make other changes here and there. I'll improve the shining hour by putting in a little bit here and taking out something there. In the heel of the hunt, you probably won't recognise yourself. Now, Miss Dolan, I'd like to ask you some questions, if I may — some personal details.

MOLLIE: Personal details. You must be out of your tiny Chinese mind if you think I'm going to answer questions on personal matters, Mr. ... — I don't think I've heard your surname.

MICHAEL: Carroll is the name. The questions I have in mind are just simple questions on factual matters. For example, what age are you, Miss Dolan?

MOLLIE: What age am I? Why, a policeman wouldn't ask me that.

MICHAEL: It's a very simple question. There's no mystery about it and you should be able to give me a simple answer.

MOLLIE: The simple reason is it's no affair of a stranger like you what age I am.

MICHAEL: Seemingly it's no concern of your two friends here

either. I believe neither Ann nor Kate know your age.

MOLLIE: Perhaps not, but if they ever wish to ask me, I'll have no hesitation in telling them.

MICHAEL: All right, we'll say you're around the forty mark, although you look much younger. Well then, a few more simple factual questions. Where do you hail from originally, Miss Dolan?

MOLLIE: Not that it's any business of yours, Mr. Carroll, but I happen to come from County Tipp.

MICHAEL: Father's occupation?

MOLLIE: My father had the honour to be a school principal. Likewise my mother. Again not that it's any business of yours, Mr. Carroll.

MICHAEL: Well then, Miss Dolan, here's a highly revealing question. When did you last spend a holiday in a nudist camp?

ANN: Now, Michael, you're carrying the joke too far.

KATE: Yes, Michael, give over.

MOLLIE: I'm glad to see you're both of the same mind as myself about this line of questioning, inflicted on me by this quite extraordinary individual. Nudist camp, indeed! Do you normally go around asking girls questions like that, Mr. Carroll? I have never been so insulted in all my born days.

MICHAEL: I don't see it as an insult. Just a factual question.

MOLLIE: Insult or not I don't intend wasting my time talking to a stranger like you.

MICHAEL: *[springing the question on her suddenly]* Miss Dolan, what are you trying to hide?

MOLLIE: What makes you think I have something to hide?

MICHAEL: Oh, now, a little bird tells me. . . .

MOLLIE: I'm sure we all have something or other we'd rather not hear shouted from the roof tops. Come to think of it, Mr. Carroll, what are you trying to hide?

ANN: Yes, Michael, there's a good question.

MOLLIE: No reply from Mr. Carroll. Well, then we'll assume he has quite a lot to hide and leave it at that. For myself, I've more important matters to discuss — with my two room mates. *[to Ann and Kate]* Now, girls, I've news for you. You are about to acquire a new room mate. A new girl will be coming here shortly.

ANN: *[a bit perplexed]* Another girl?

KATE: Who is she? Where are we going to put her?

MOLLIE: She's a very nice girl I met down in the Girls' Club. Margaret Finnegan is her name. She had to leave home suddenly in Galway because of a row between herself and her parents and she came to Dublin with only a few pounds in her pocket. I don't know how she found her way to the Club but, anyway, I've been able to fix her up with a job in a grocer's shop through a friend of mine. But she has no proper digs as yet.

KATE: There's no room for another girl here.

ANN: We're congested enough as it is.

MOLLIE: It will be only for a few months until she finds her feet. Where is your charity, girls?

MICHAEL: There's a good question, girls — where is your charity?

MOLLIE: That is none of your business, Mr. Carroll.

ANN: Where is she going to sleep?

KATE: Yes, where will she sleep?

MOLLIE: Well, there's no room for an extra person in my little room. There isn't room to swing the proverbial cat in it as it is. There's nothing for it but to push her in somehow with the two of you.

KATE: But can't you see that we have barely enough room as it is. We don't want to make a proper tenement of the place, now do we?

MOLLIE: Tenement? Don't exaggerate.

KATE: O.K., you give me a better name for it.

MOLLIE: *[cuttingly]* Yes, I suppose you would know all about tenements and overcrowding and that kind of thing. You should be quite an authority on it, I should think. Five brothers and three sisters you have, isn't it?

KATE: Where or how I was raised has nothing to do with the matter and is my business, not yours.

MICHAEL: That's the girl, Kate. Give it to her, straight from the shoulder.

ANN: Now, now, girls, we're getting away from the matter in hand. All we are concerned with at this moment in time is whether there's room for another girl here and I say there is not.

51

KATE: And I second that.

MOLLIE: *[conciliatingly]* What's involved, girls, is only a couple of months, I guarantee. Granted, it means a little inconvenience but with the right will it can be done. If it is necessary to put ourselves out a little from time to time in this world, be assured that we will get our reward with interest in the world to come. Now as a Christian gesture, can we not take this girl in for a couple of months?

ANN: *[with bad grace]* Oh, all right, have it your way.

KATE: But mind it is only for two months — not a day more.

MICHAEL: You said there was some kind of friction between this girl and her parents. Could you elaborate on that aspect, please?

MOLLIE: Not that it is any concern of yours, Mr. Carroll, but my two flat mates have a right to know. I believe the nub of the problem was that her parents were trying to marry this girl Margaret off to a man more than twice her age. But Margaret apparently had other ideas.

MICHAEL: *[half to himself]* I can see that this Margaret is an independent-minded, spirited kind of girl. The very kind of character I need to act as a kind of catalyst. Well, it will be interesting to see how she reacts on this lot. *[to the girls]* Well, I may as well be off. Good-bye, girls. Miss Dolan! *[with an elaborate bow]* I'll surely have a play for you before long.

ANN/KATE: *[together]* Goodbye, Michael. *[Michael exits as the curtain falls.]*

SCENE 2

The same — some weeks later

ANN: *[coming in door Right carrying hold-all]* Yoo-hoo! Anyone at home?

KATE: *[from kitchenette]* I'm in here, Ann. Welcome back to the big smoke. *[Enter Kate]*

ANN: Big smoke is right. *[She puts hold-all in corner and takes off overcoat]*

KATE: Will I put the kettle on for you?

ANN: No, thanks Kate. I had a bite on the train coming up.

KATE: Had a nice week-end, I suppose?

ANN: It was quiet but, as you know, that's how I like it.

KATE: Anyway it's a change from the city.

ANN: You can say that again. I don't know why, Kate, I always feel so miserable every time I come back into the city after a spell in the country. It's just like the first time I arrived here, a raw country girl. Did you ever notice, Kate, coming in on the train from the West, first you leave the lush green fields of Meath and Kildare behind you and pass through the new housing estates on the outskirts of the city. Then the houses begin to get older and shabbier and suddenly, coming near Amiens Street, you find yourself bang in the middle of the tenements and the mean, tattered heart of this city . . . Sometimes I ask myself is it worthwhile going home at all.

KATE: I suppose we always remain country girls at heart. *[resignedly]* However, it won't take long for you to get back into the same old rut again.

ANN: "The same old rut" is right! But maybe it's no harm that we should be jogged out of that old rut from time to time so that we realise the size of the rut we've got ourselves into.

KATE: Ah, but sure maybe it's not that bad. Things are never so bad they couldn't be worse.

ANN: There's nothing worse than boredom. I often think of the three of us here and how we are slowly but inevitably going to seed. We came to the city ten, fifteen, twenty years ago full of hope and great expectations. But we allowed this monster of a city to swallow us up and what have we got to show for the wasted years?

KATE: You're in fine fettle this evening, Ann. It must be all that talk of Margaret's about her native parts that's gone to your head. That native valley of hers with the sun going down behind the hills, the lark in the clear air, the mist that does be on the bog, all that mush!

ANN: Maybe there's a certain amount of exaggeration in what Margaret says about her native place but there's a grain of truth there too . . . But that's enough of that for this evening. I suppose Mollie hasn't come back yet.

KATE: No. She's usually that bit later than you in getting back, not being dependent on public transport like you and me.

ANN: Nothing strange or startling, I suppose.

KATE: Yes, indeed. Something happened in this flat over the weekend that happens only rarely.

ANN: I think I know. You had a man here, or was it men?

KATE: Singular, I regret to say.

ANN: Who was it? — not that drip, Michael.

KATE: No. Guess again.

ANN: It must be Margaret then. That fellow she has down the country.

KATE: The very man. He was up for the weekend and they went to a match in Croke Park and she brought him over here for tea. Then off for a few drinks and a hop afterwards.

ANN: What's he like?

KATE: A fine, big, strapping fellow. A bit rough and ready, maybe, for our citified tastes.

ANN: And the inevitable question — what does he do?

KATE: He's some kind of a contractor, as far as I can make out.

ANN: A contractor, by Dad!

KATE: In a small way. He has a tractor and farm machinery and he does work for farmers. I don't know what Mollie is going to say when she hears he was here.

ANN: There's no reason why she should hear a word about it, for God's sake. Neither of us are going to split on Margaret, now, are we?

KATE: If we don't tell Mollie, there's someone else who will. I mean Miss Shine. As ill luck would have it, Margaret and boyfriend bumped into her coming through the hall.

ANN: Is it possible to do anything unknown to that old bags? As you say, Mollie is going to hear all about your man. I wonder did Margaret know about this famous rule of ours.

KATE: Certainly, she knows all about it. But she decided to take a chance.

ANN: Poor old Margaret, I'm afraid she's for it then. By the way, any news of our playwright friend?

KATE: Don't I see him in the office every day.

ANN: He's still intent on writing that play, I suppose.

KATE: He says the idea is coming along nicely, but he hasn't exactly got down to writing it yet. He'll be coming here again, he says — in particular he wants to see Margaret. He

54

says he's thinking of calling the play "the Country Girls".

ANN: As a title that seems apt enough.

KATE: I'm beginning to wonder was it wise drawing him on us at all.

ANN: Sure, it's a bit of gas. It keeps life from getting too dull. When I think of the questions he asked poor old Mollie.

KATE: Oh then, poor old Mollie was well able for him.

ANN: But that question about the nudist camp, that was really going beyond the beyonds. Such a question to ask her and she about the most unlikely client for a nudist camp you could meet. *[They both laugh]*

KATE: And the look of astonishment that Mollie put on. She nearly fell out of her standing she was so absolutely flabbergasted.

ANN: But joking apart, that fellow must have the cheek of the devil. Did I hear the front door bang?

KATE: That will be her ladyship, I suppose. *[reverting to Michael]* He says, of course, that he asks girls the most awful questions on purpose, so that he can study their reactions. Something to do with psychology. *[Enter Mollie carrying small suitcase]*

MOLLIE: Hello, girls. I'm back.

KATE: You had a nice time, I suppose. Ann has only just got in before you.

MOLLIE: Yes, I had a nice, quiet time. But rather sad. Father is, as you know, well on in years now and, leaving home, one is never sure if it is the last one will see of him. And mother isn't really able to cope with an old person like that any more. It would cost the world to get someone to look after him. Not like the old days when servant girls were two a penny. But you can't get the youth to take jobs like that anymore. Sure, the likes of them are all working in the Civil Service now, I suppose. Was it Horace who said "tempora mutanter"? However, that's enough of my woes ... I'm absolutely dying for a cigarette. I left my lighter behind me at home. Where's the matches, does anyone know?

KATE: The matches are in the kitchen.

MOLLIE: *[as she exits towards kitchenette]* I may as well put on the kettle while I'm at it. I could do with a cup of tea.

KATE: She's on the servant girls theme again. What was it that bloke Horace said?

ANN: Tempora mutanter! *[They are both laughing when Mollie returns suddenly. She is carrying an ask tray.]*

MOLLIE: *[excitedly]* Some one was smoking a lot around here. What's this in the name of fortune? Tobacco ash. I'd know it anywhere. My father is a pipe man, you know. Kate, you had a man or possibly men here at the weekend.

KATE: I suppose you were bound to find out sooner or later. Yes, Margaret brought her man in here yesterday evening.

MOLLIE: Did she now? Wasn't that very adjacent?

KATE: It was all above board, I guarantee you.

ANN: Yes, Kate was acting as chaperone.

MOLLIE: That's not the point. I must speak to Margaret about this.

ANN: Don't be too hard on her, Mollie. She didn't mean to do any harm.

MOLLIE: She broke a rule of this flat — the most important rule we have.

KATE: Look, she only took him in for tea in broad daylight.

MOLLIE: I don't care whether it was broad daylight or not. There's a principle at stake and I consider that Margaret has taken quite a liberty. And after all I did for that girl. I took her in charge when she was down and out. I got her a job — admittedly, not much of a job but the best she could expect with her standard of education. We took her in here at great inconvenience to us all. And after all that, the first chance she gets she brings in her man. She has taken a liberty and I intend to have it out with her. However, I must go and unpack. *[She exits through door Right with suitcase]*

ANN: It looks as if Margaret is going to get it hot and heavy. And we have to admit that Mollie did a lot for her. But I always thought that Margaret has a devilishly independent streak in her.

KATE: You can say that again. Look at the way she defied her parents when they were trying to marry her to that old fellow back home.

ANN: And left them all high and dry so that she could be true to her grá geal a croí. *[They both laugh]*

KATE: It's like something out of a book.

ANN: We shouldn't be making fun of her. If we only had a little of her spunk ourselves. *[The front door is heard banging]* There she blows!

KATE: Like a lamb to the slaughter. *[Enter Margaret, a good-looking girl in her mid twenties. She wears jeans.]*

MARGARET: Hello, girls.

ANN AND KATE: Hi, Margaret!

MARGARET: Welcome back, Ann.

ANN: Thanks, Margaret. I hear you had a high old time of it when Mollie and I were away.

MARGARET: Kate was telling you all the news, I suppose. I hope you didn't mention it to Mollie.

KATE: There was no necessity. As ill luck would have it your fellow left his trade mark behind him and Private Eye Mollie wasn't long in noting it.

MARGARET: What do you mean, trade mark?

ANN: He left a lot of pipe ash behind him, Margaret. That would make a good title for a thriller. "The mystery of the pipe ash".

KATE: Or Inspector Mollie blows her top!

[They all laugh. Mollie returns suddenly.]

MOLLIE: I'm glad, girls, you find something so unspeakably funny. Perhaps I, too, could take part in the general hilarity — if I only knew what it's all about.

MARGARET: Ah, sure, there was nothing very funny at all.

MOLLIE: Laughing at my expense, I expect you were.

ANN: Not at all, Mollie. Laughing at the pipe ash we were.

MOLLIE: Yes, Margaret, I understand that while my back was turned, you took it on yourself to break one of the most important rules of this flat.

MARGARET: All right, Mollie. There's no need to beat about the bush. I brought Liam in for tea yesterday. I don't see anything terribly wrong in that. Yourself and Ann were away and Kate didn't mind. I don't see why it should annoy you so much.

MOLLIE: That's not the point. You knew the rule was there and you should not have broken it.

MARGARET: But there's really no sense in that old rule.

MOLLIE: No, sense in it. Well, I never! Listen, young lady, I don't think you are in any position to make a remark like that. I'll have you know that this rule was only adopted after long and bitter experience of sharing flats with girls in various parts of this city and the trouble and inconvenience invariably caused by girls bringing in their boy friends.

MARGARET: It's a wonder you never thought of going into a bedsitter on you own then. It would solve all your problems.

MOLLIE: Are you presuming to tell me what I should do?

KATE: Margaret is only making what appears to be quite a sensible suggestion.

MOLLIE: On the contrary, she is presuming to tell me what I should do. There's the thanks after all I did for her.

MARGARET: Look, Mollie, it's not that I'm ungrateful to you. I don't know what would have become of me if it wasn't for you. But I can't allow you to run my life.

MOLLIE: I have no desire to do any such thing.

MARGARET: But that's what you're trying to do indirectly. And after what you've done with your own life!

MOLLIE: For your information and to all whom it may concern, I did with my life precisely what I wanted to do with it. But maybe you're so ignorant as to assume that there's something radically wrong with a girl unless she has two or three fellows in tow.

KATE: That's not what Margaret meant at all.

MOLLIE: Don't you be sticking your nose into what doesn't concern you or I'll deal with you in the same way as I'm going to deal with this innocent.

KATE: And what way is that, Miss High and Mighty?

MOLLIE: Any person that breaks an important rule like this — there's only one punishment that meets the crime. She'll have to leave.

ANN: But you can't throw her out just like that. She has no where else to go.

MOLLIE: She should have thought of that before she brought her precious boy friend in here. She has to go quite soon anyway. We took her in on a strictly temporary basis — remember?

KATE: Personally, I want Margaret to stay as long as she likes — or at least until she gets fixed up somewhere else.

MARGARET: Could I say something that might help to solve the situation? I don't expect to be staying very long anyway.

58

Liam and myself are on the look-out for a house back in Galway and as soon as we find one, we'll be getting married, please God. I don't think I could bear much more of this jungle of a city anyway, where people walk in fear and dread in broad daylight on the main streets, where robbery, rape and mugging are everyday occurrences. As far as I'm concerned, you can have your Dublin. It's the country life for me. Back to God's fresh air, away from the noise and the bustle and the pollution and the traffic jams.

[Michael comes in door Right suddenly]

MICHAEL: I found the front door open, so I took the liberty of coming straight up.

KATE: Michael, you've come at the psychological moment as they say.

MOLLIE: Without invitation, of course, Mr. Carroll.

MICHAEL: Don't mind me. Pray continue. From what I could hear coming up the stairs, things were hotting up towards a crisis.

MOLLIE: This simpleton has broken one of the most important rules of the flat.

MICHAEL: Don't tell me she had the temerity to bring a man in here. Didn't I tell you that she has all the marks of a catalyst?

KATE: [sarcastically] A catalyst is all we need!

ANN: Well, Michael, how is the play coming along?

MICHAEL: It's coming along nicely, Ann. But I may have to jazz things up a bit so as to make it more compelling from the audience's point of view. I've had to ask myself some pointed questions about some of the characters. Are they all they appear on the surface? If we delve beneath the surface, are there any startling revelations? Take Mollie, for example — I mean Miss Dolan. Could there be in her past some unhappy love affair? Could this explain her extraordinary antipathy to men?

MOLLIE: I would thank you to mind your own business, Mr. Carroll.

MICHAEL: But it is my business as a dramatist to delve into my characters' past.

MOLLIE: Well, you'll do no delving into mine.

MICHAEL: How come, Miss Dolan? Is there some nasty little secret lurking there?—something you thought you had lived down? Does the name George Kenny ring a bell, Miss Dolan?

MOLLIE: That is my affair, Mr. Carroll.

MICHAEL: Your affair indeed. A rather unfortunate choice of words, don't you think, Miss Dolan? — since Mr. Kenny was a married man.

MOLLIE: I didn't know that when I went out with him first.

MICHAEL: But when you did find it out, you continued meeting him.

MOLLIE: We were very much in love at that stage.

MICHAEL: *You* were very much in love, Miss Dolan. But not George. He was only playing around with you.

MOLLIE: He had to choose between me and his wife and children.

MICHAEL: And he chose the latter, Miss Dolan. And left you holding the baby, did he not? It was something you didn't hold for very long, it should be added, for you took the easy way out. George Kenny was, of course, decent enough to pay for your [*meaningly*] little operation, was he not?

MOLLIE: [*angrily*] Listen, Mr. Carroll, I'm not discussing this matter any further with you.

MICHAEL: Yes, perhaps we've discussed it enough.

MOLLIE: I think it shocking that someone deliberately prys into another person's private affairs.

ANN: Michael, I think you've overstepped the mark this time.

MICHAEL: Put it down to my relentless search for truth.

MOLLIE: You just want to drive me out of this flat, Mr. Carroll, for reasons best known to yourself. You wanted to make my situation untenable vis-a-vis the other girls. You will be glad to know you have succeeded. I hope you feel pleased with yourself. I'll be leaving as soon as ever I can find myself another place.

ANN: I'd like you to know, Mollie, that Michael's revelations about you make no difference to me. I see no reason why you should feel yourself compelled to leave.

MOLLIE: It's decent of you to say so, Ann, but things could never be the same again between us after the way this monster has shown me up. I have a splitting headache. Excuse me! [*She exits suddenly at door Right.*]

[*There is an uncomfortable pause following Mollie's exit.*]

ANN: Michael, I do feel you had no right to show her up the way you've just done.

MICHAEL: As a dramatist it's my job to delve beneath the surface. I warned you, when I undertook to write this play, that I'd be making some searching enquiries about my characters.

MARGARET: Mollie to you is only a character in a play then.

ANN: But to the rest of us she's flesh and blood — a person in other words.

MICHAEL: She's flesh and blood to me too, very much so. But I have to look at her with a certain amount of clinical detachment.

KATE: How did you manage to get this information about her anyway?

MICHAEL: Just one of those coincidences that life seems to be so full of. This is a small town. There may happen to be a million people in it but it's a small town. Actually, I happen to know her ex-lover, George Kenny.

ANN: And the rotter had nothing better to do than spill the beans to you, I suppose.

MICHAEL: In a moment of drunken confidentiality.

MARGARET: I feel a bit of a heel for my part in the whole business. And after all she did for me.

MICHAEL: You need not feel badly about it all, Margaret. After all, if it weren't for my revelations about her, 'tis you'd be going out the door, not her.

KATE: Don't worry, Margaret. She'll get a nice little bedsitter all to herself.

MICHAEL: Where she can make all the silly rules she likes. Which reminds me, Kate, I've just invested in a second-hand typewriter. Maybe, if I brought it over here some evening you could give me lessons on how to type.

KATE: Sure, it's all practice, Michael, as long as you start on the right foot.

MICHAEL: That's precisely what I want you to show me — how to start on the right foot, or to be more precise, on the right fingers.

KATE: [jokingly] I'm afraid my fee is quite high, Michael. I don't know could you afford it.

MICHAEL: Go on with you now! The fee for this assignment

will be quite nominal but the perks will be out of this world.

KATE: Such as —

MICHAEL: Oh, now, I haven't quite made up my mind on that score. Suffice to say, the odd dinner dance, the odd play, the odd film. This could really build up into something big.

ANN: I do believe, Kate, he's talking about doing a line with you.

KATE: You don't know that fellow, Ann. He's probably having me on in a big way. I'll believe that dinner dance when I see it.

MARGARET: Anyway, let him bring over his old typewriter and take it from there.

MICHAEL: A sound idea, my bonnie catalyst. I'll bring over my typewriter, my charming postman's daughter, and we'll leave the rest in the lap of the gods.

ANN: *[as she glances into kitchenette]* The kettle is boiling now. Let's have a nice cup of tea. *[There is a general air of hilarity as the curtain falls]*

CURTAIN